THIS BOOK BELONGS TO:

YOU MIGHT ALSO NEED

Small Print Handwriting Workbook for Kids:
Improve your Penmanship with
151 Fascinating Facts
about History, Science, and More

GET THE BOOK

The Print Handwriting Workbook for Teens:
Improve your Penmanship and Writing Skills
with Motivational & Inspirational Quotes for
Young Adults

GET THE BOOK

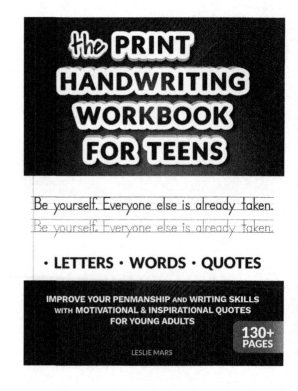

YOU MIGHT ALSO NEED

The Print Handwriting Workbook for Kids:
Improve your Penmanship
with 101 Interesting
Science Facts

GET THE BOOK

Print Handwriting Workbook for Teens:
Improve your Penmanship
with Facts about 52 Remarkable Women
who Changed the World

GET THE BOOK

Introduction

Welcome to the *Print Handwriting Workbook for Teens*! This workbook is for teens who are looking to learn or improve their print penmanship skills with facts about 52 great scientists who changed the world.

Discover amazing facts about various scientists who made history and put a dent in the universe. Learn more about scientific discoveries and improve your handwriting at the same time. The figures presented in this book cover regions all over the world. Each featured figure has made significant contributions in their respective fields, from physics, engineering, and computer science to astronomy, biology, chemistry, geology and much more. Writing short facts about their lives and achievements takes you an unforgettable and educational journey.

In this workbook, you will find various writing exercises in a legal ruled font-size designed for teens.

- The first part begins with the alphabet where letters are practiced through tracing and connecting the dots. Each letter is presented with directional arrows to guide the hand movements as you learn, while also improving your handwriting.

- The second part moves on to writing facts about 52 Scientists who changed the world, such as: Albert Einstein, Ada Lovelace, Charles Darwin, Lise Meitner, Hippocrates, Hypatia, Stephen Hawking and many more. You will gain thorough practice in writing words first, which are extracted from the fact with a traceable printing font. The next step moves on to writing the entire sentence from the fact multiple times.

It may seem tedious at first, but trust that print handwriting will help establish the tenacity that is important for your many learning experiences throughout life.

PRINT HANDWRITING WORKBOOK FOR TEENS:

Improve your Penmanship with Facts About
52 Great Scientists who Changed the World

WHAT'S INSIDE?

A FEW TIPS:

- Good posture is essential during writing. Sitting upright with feet flat on the floor will help with your writing efficiency.

- B Pencils are softer, ensuring smoother and more effortless writing. You may likewise start practicing printing with ink pens once proficiency with the letters has been achieved.

- Feel free to cut out and copy any page in the book to continue your handwriting practice.

- Be patient! Improving your handwriting is a journey of learning and growth. Remember, nothing of real value is ever easy.

UPPERCASE LETTERS

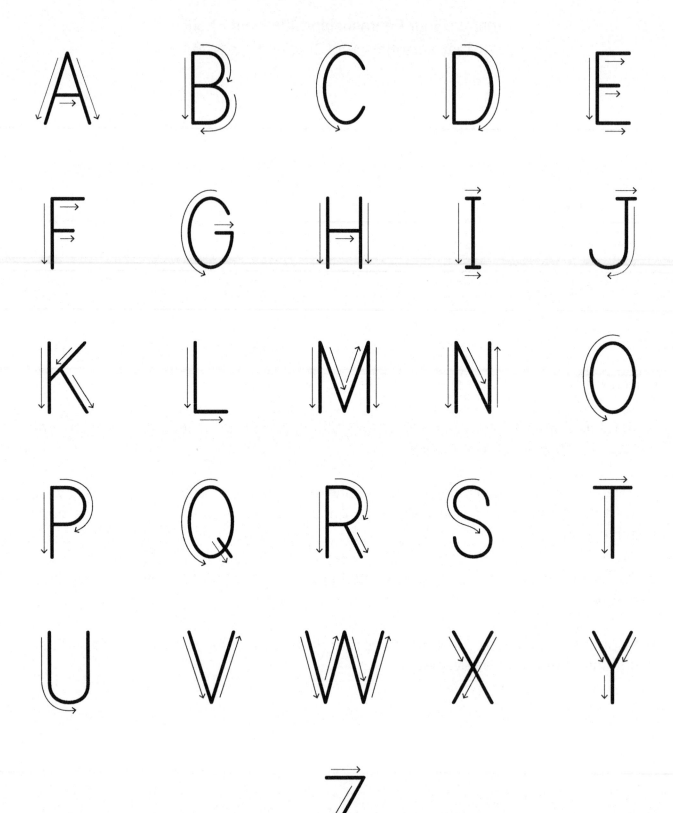

LOWERCASE LETTERS

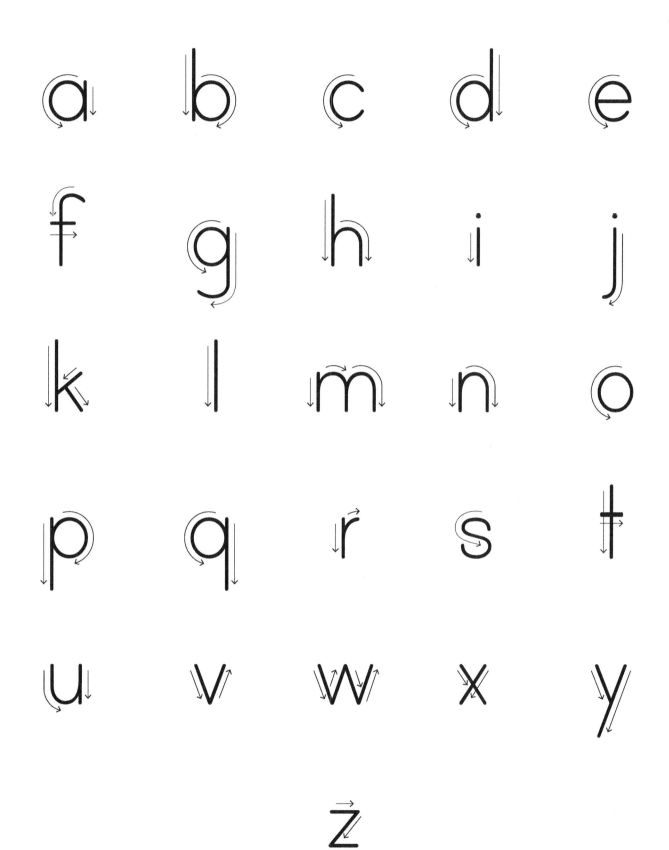

Jane Cooke Wright

Hypatia

Alfred Nobel

Ada Lovelace

Nikola Tesla

Marie Curie

Charles Darwin

Leonardo Da Vinci

Mileva Maric

Sir Isaac Newton

Part 1:

Letters

Trace the dotted letters and then write the letters on your own.

A A A A A A A A

A A A A A A A A

A A A A A A A A

A A A A A A A A

A

A

A

A

a a a a a a a a

a a a a a a a a

a a a a a a a a

a a a a a a a a

a

a

a

a

B   B   B   B   B   B   B
B   B   B   B   B   B   B
B   B   B   B   B   B   B
B   B   B   B   B   B   B

B
B
B
B

b   b   b   b   b   b   b
b   b   b   b   b   b   b
b   b   b   b   b   b   b
b   b   b   b   b   b   b

b
b
b
b

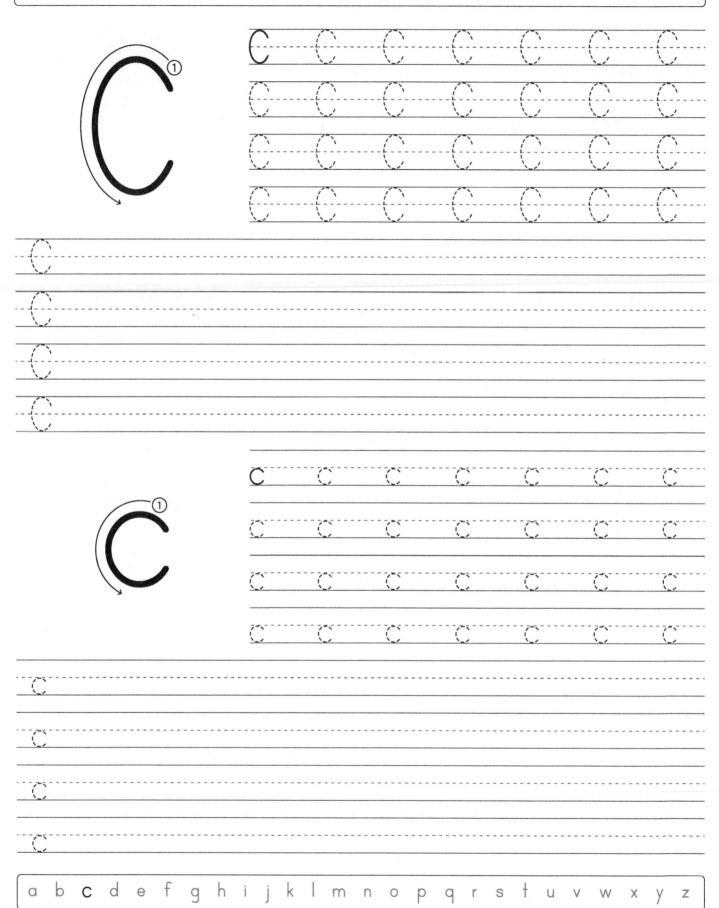

D

D D D D D D D

d

d d d d d d d

A B C D **E** F G H I J K L M N O P Q R S T U V W X Y Z

E

e

a b c d **e** f g h i j k l m n o p q r s t u v w x y z

9

F

f

G   G   G   G   G   G   G

G   G   G   G   G   G   G

G   G   G   G   G   G   G

G   G   G   G   G   G   G

G

G

G

G

g   g   g   g   g   g   g

g   g   g   g   g   g   g

g   g   g   g   g   g   g

g   g   g   g   g   g   g

g

g

g

g

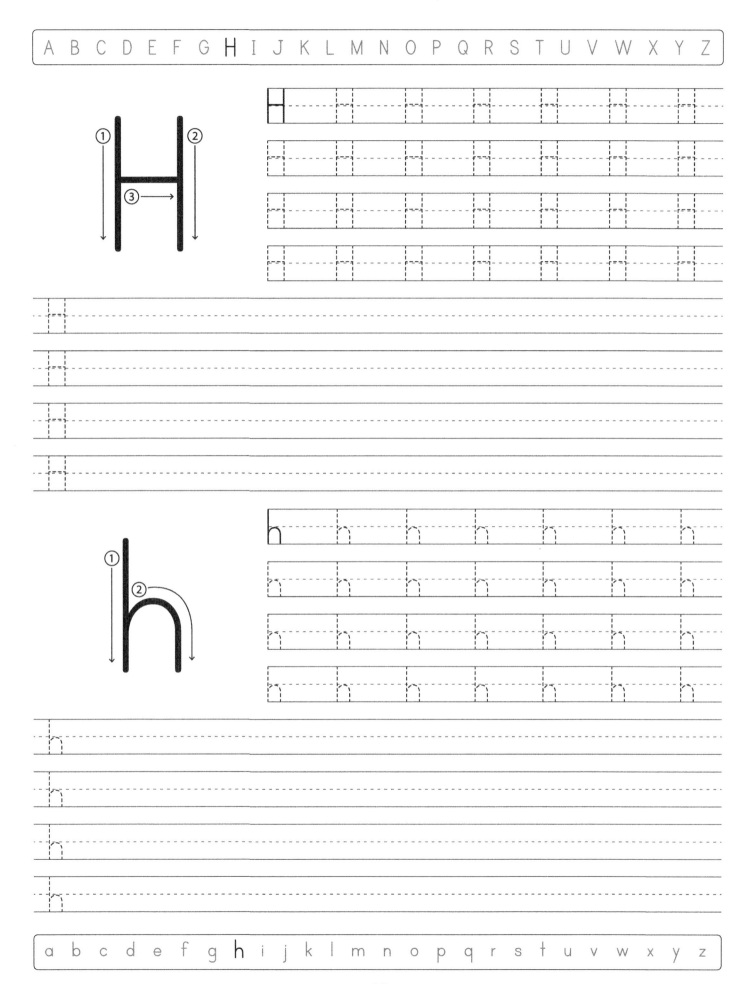

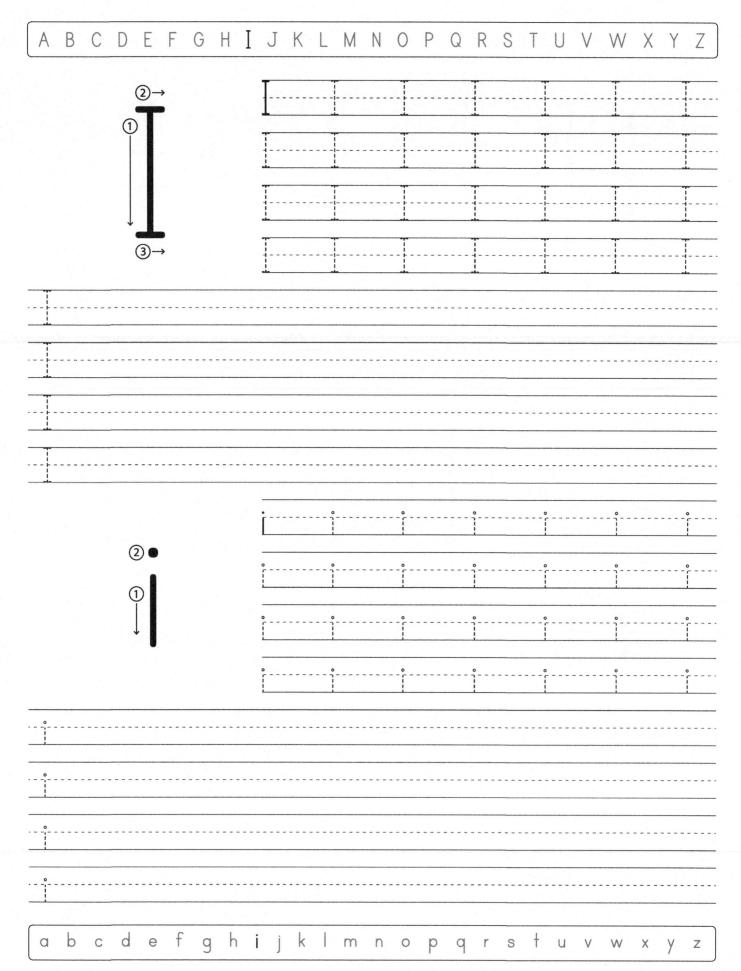

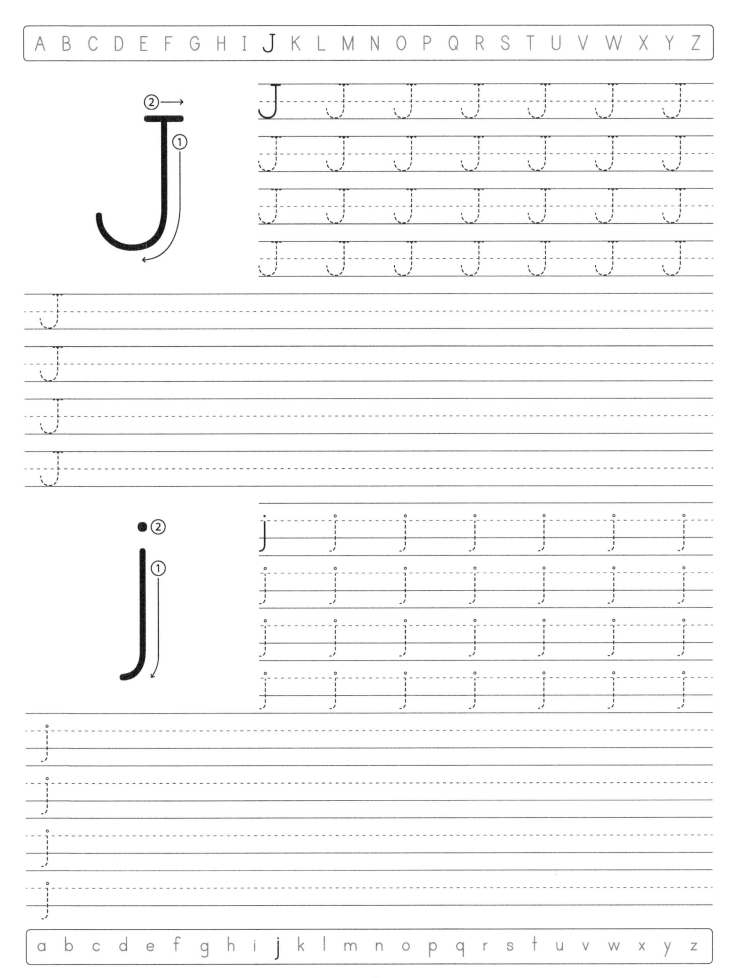

K K K K K K K

k k k k k k k

M M M M M M M

M M M M M M M

M M M M M M M

M M M M M M M

M

M

M

M

m m m m m m m

m m m m m m m

m m m m m m m

m m m m m m m

m

m

m

m

N

n

O

o

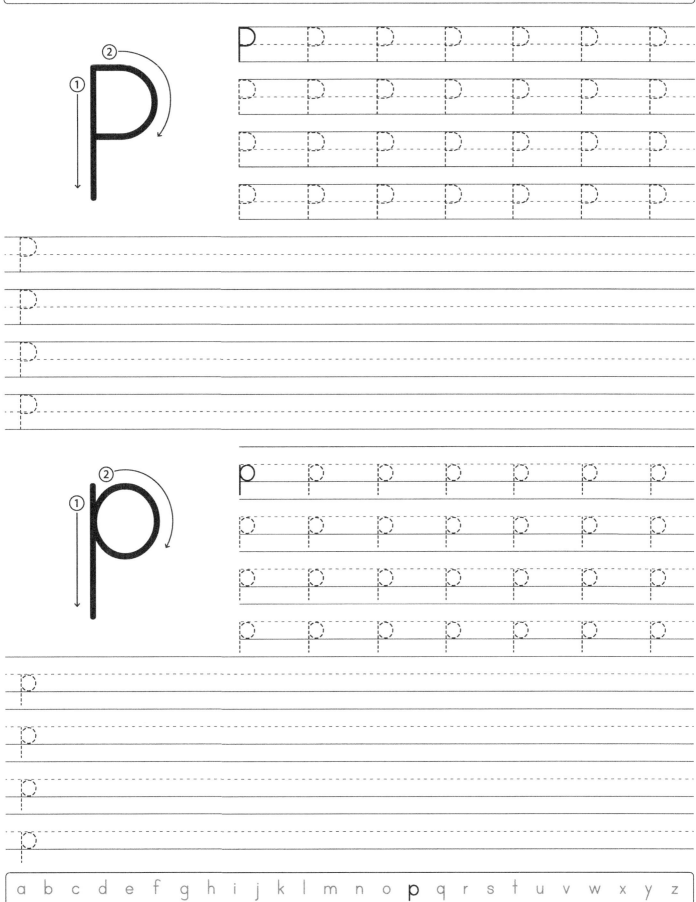

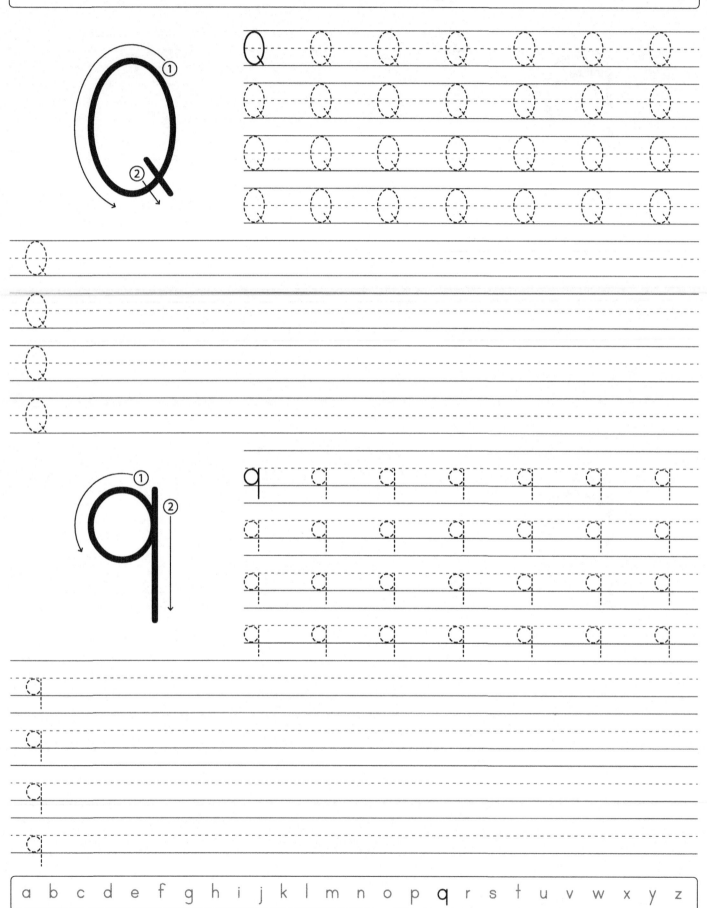

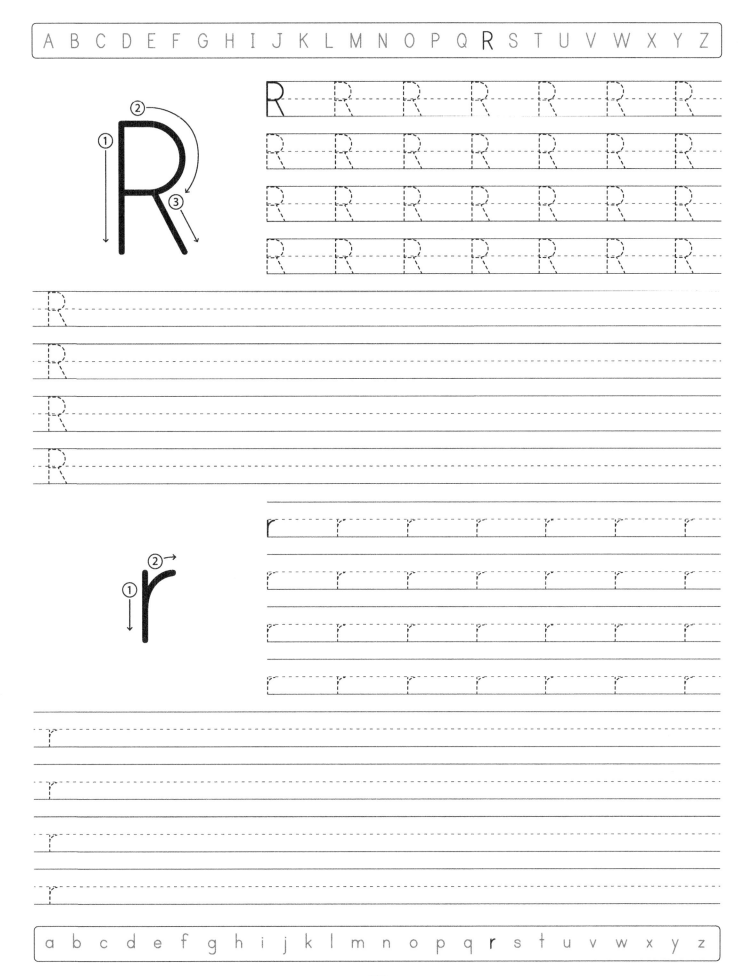

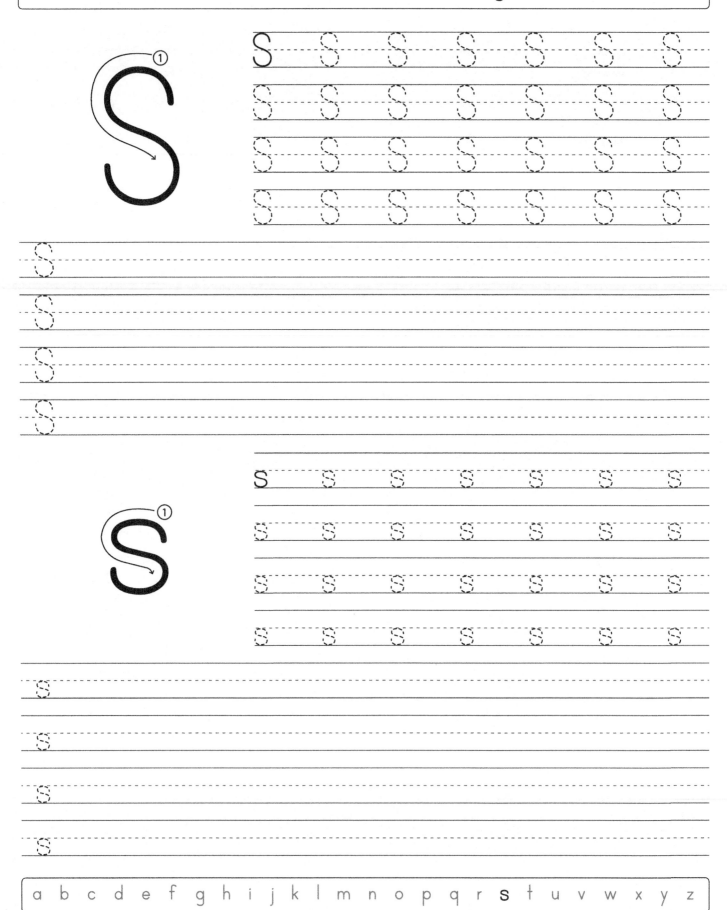

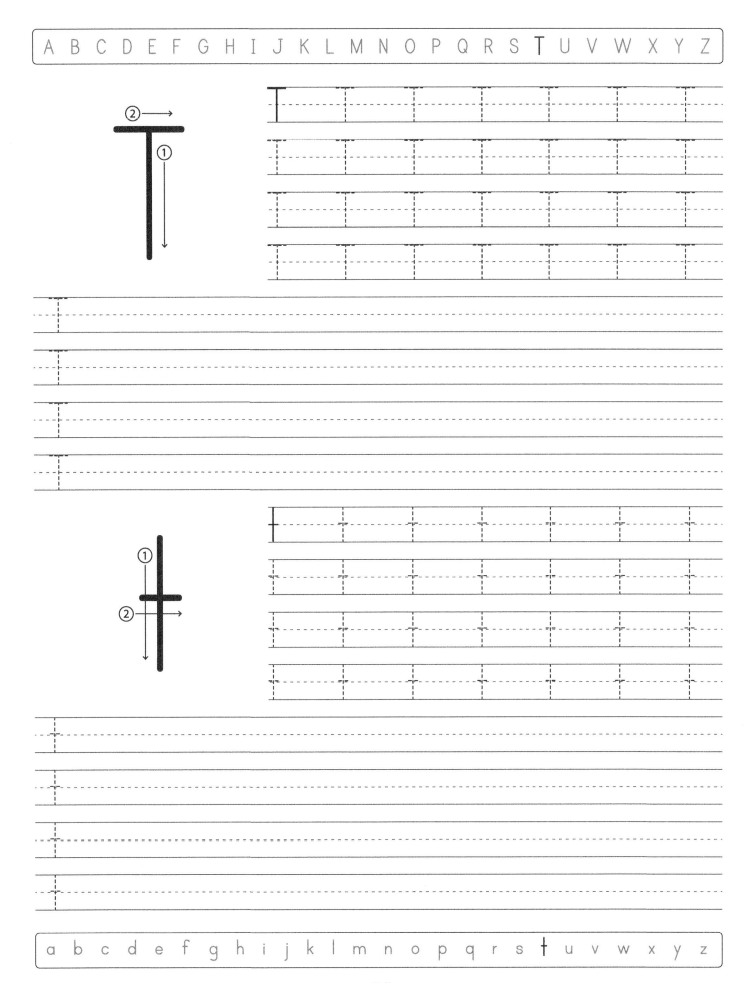

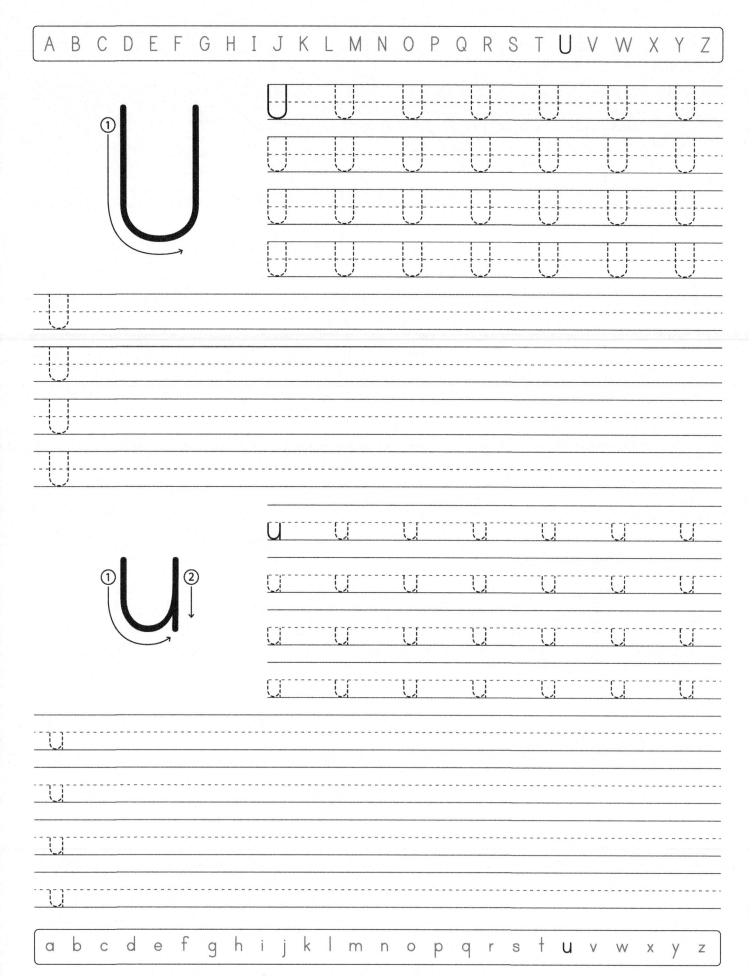

A B C D E F G H I J K L M N O P Q R S T U **V** W X Y Z

V

a b c d e f g h i j k l m n o p q r s t u **v** w x y z

26

W W W W W W W

W W W W W W W

W W W W W W W

W W W W W W W

W

W

W

W

W W W W W W W

W W W W W W W

W W W W W W W

W W W W W W W

w

w

w

w

A B C D E F G H I J K L M N O P Q R S T U V W X Y Z

a b c d e f g h i j k l m n o p q r s t u v w x y z

28

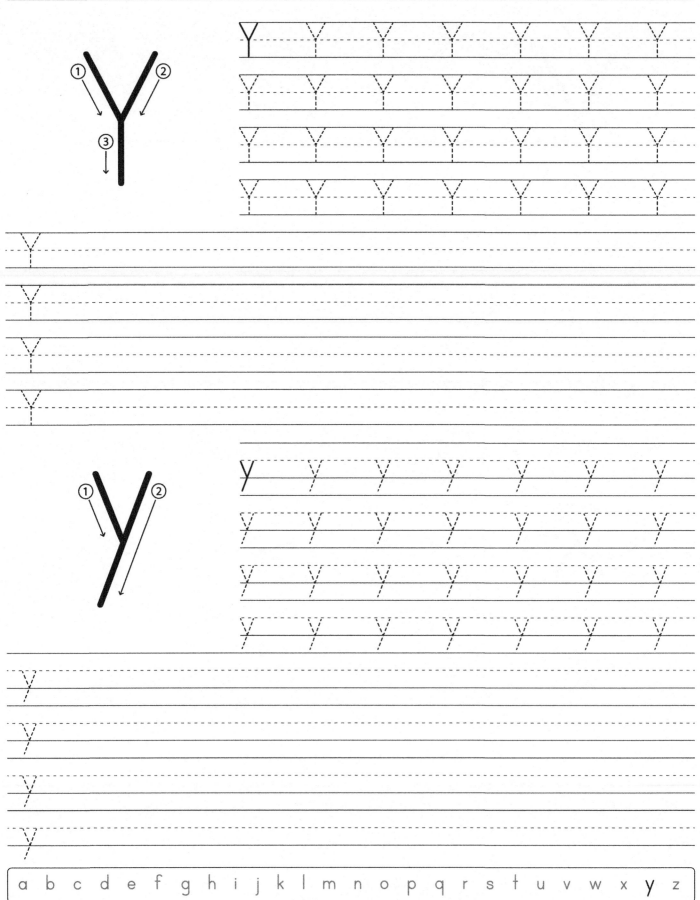

Z Z Z Z Z Z Z

z z z z z z z

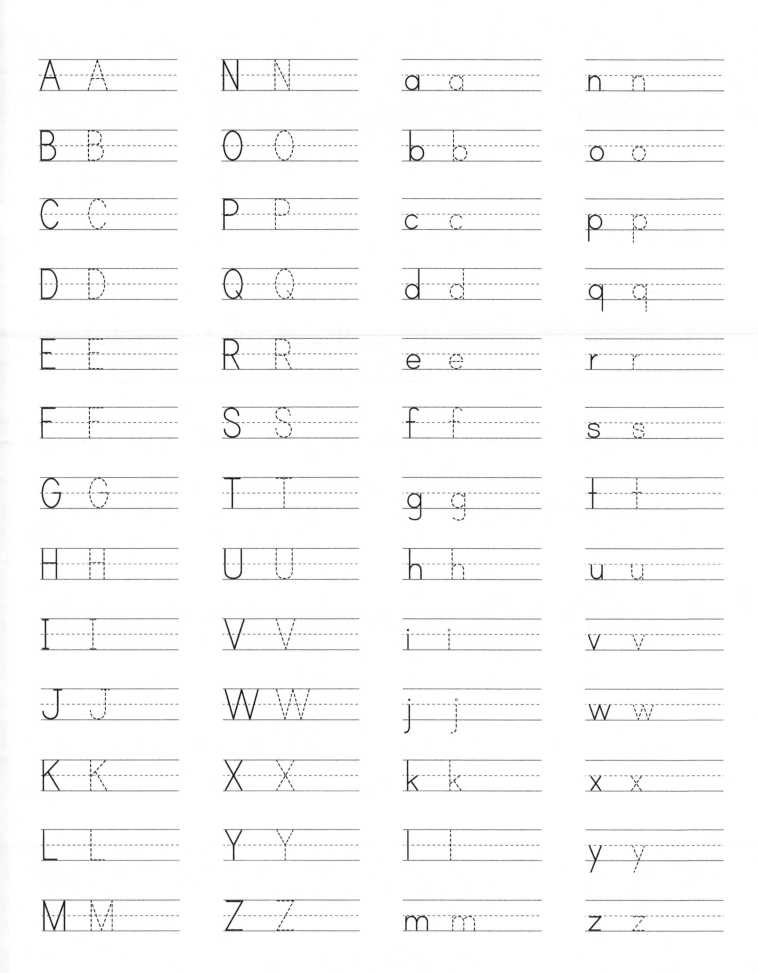

Part 2:

Facts

Trace the dotted words and sentences, then write them on your own.

Pythagoras
c. 570 BC - c. 490 BC

Pythagoras is famous for developing the "Pythagorean Theorem" equation.

Pythagoras is   Pythagoras is

famous for   famous for

developing the   developing the

"Pythagorean   "Pythagorean

Theorem"   Theorem"

equation.   equation.

Pythagoras is famous for developing the
"Pythagorean Theorem" equation.

Pythagoras is famous for developing the
"Pythagorean Theorem" equation.

Pythagoras is famous for developing the
"Pythagorean Theorem" equation.

Ada Lovelace
1815-1852

Ada Lovelace was a mathematician and the first computer programmer.

Ada Lovelace   Ada Lovelace

was a   was a

mathematician mathematician

and the first   and the first

computer   computer

programmer.   programmer.

Ada Lovelace was a mathematician and
the first computer programmer.
Ada Lovelace was a mathematician and
the first computer programmer.
Ada Lovelace was a mathematician and
the first computer programmer.

Hypatia
c.355-c.415

Hypatia was a famous female mathematician and a popular teacher throughout Alexandria, Egypt.

Hypatia was a

famous female

mathematician

and a popular

teacher throughout

Alexandria, Egypt.

Hypatia was a famous female mathematician and a popular teacher throughout Alexandria, Egypt.

Hypatia was a famous female mathematician and a popular teacher throughout Alexandria, Egypt.

James Chadwick
1891-1974

Discovered the neutron and led the
British scientists who worked on the
Manhattan Project.

Discovered the

Discovered the

neutron and

neutron and

led the British

led the British

scientists who

scientists who

worked on the

worked on the

Manhattan Project.

Manhattan Project.

Discovered the neutron and led the British
scientists who worked on the Manhattan
Project.

Discovered the neutron and led the British
scientists who worked on the Manhattan
Project.

Robert Boyle
1627-1691

Robert Boyle is one of the founders of modern chemistry, most known for "Boyle's Law."

Robert Boyle

is one of the

founders

modern chemistry,

most known

for "Boyle's Law."

Robert Boyle is one of the founders of
modern chemistry, most known for
"Boyle's Law."
Robert Boyle is one of the founders of
modern chemistry most known for
"Boyle's Law.

Jane Cooke Wright

1919-2013

Dr. Jane Cooke Wright invented new ways of administering chemotherapy to those suffering from cancer.

Dr. Jane Cooke

Wright invented new

ways of administering

chemotherapy to

those suffering

from cancer.

Dr. Jane Cooke Wright invented new ways
of administering chemotherapy to those
suffering from cancer.

Dr. Jane Cooke Wright invented new ways
of administering chemotherapy to those
suffering from cancer.

Alexander Fleming

1881-1955

Alexander Fleming discovered penicillin,
an antibiotic that has saved countless
millions of lives.

Alexander Fleming

discovered penicillin,

an antibiotic

that has saved

countless millions

of lives.

Alexander Fleming discovered penicillin, an antibiotic that has saved countless millions of lives.

Alexander Fleming discovered penicillin, an antibiotic that has saved countless millions of lives.

Albert Einstein

1879-1955

Albert Einstein is known for his Theory of Relativity, which helps us understand the relationship of space and time.

Albert Einstein is

known for his Theory

of Relativity, which

helps us understand

the relationship of

space and time.

Albert Einstein is known for his Theory of
Relativity, which helps us understand
the relationship of space and time.
Albert Einstein is known for his Theory of
Relativity, which helps us understand the
relationship of space and time.

Sir Isaac Newton
1643 -1727

Newton discovered gravity and described it as a pulling force which keeps people on the ground, preventing them floating away.

Newton discovered

gravity and described

it as a pulling force

which keeps people on

the ground, preventing

them floating away.

Newton discovered gravity and described it as a pulling force which keep people on the ground, preventing them floating away.

Newton discovered gravity and described it as a pulling force which keep people on the ground, preventing them floating away.

Hippocrates
c. 460 BC - c. 375 BC

Known as the Father of Medicine, Hippocrates is credited for the Hippocratic Oath that modern medical professionals abide by.

Known as the Father of

Medicine, Hippocrates

is credited for the

Hippocratic Oath that

modern medical

professionals abide by.

Known as the Father of Medicine,
Hippocrates is credited for the Hippocratic
Oath that modern medical professionals
abide by.

Known as the Father of Medicine,
Hippocrates is credited for the Hippocratic
Oath that modern medical professionals
abide by.

Fibonacci

c. 1170 - c. 1245

Fibonacci introduced the modern Indian number system to the West, which ultimately allowed science and mathematics to flourish.

Fibonacci introduced the modern Indian
number system to the West, which ultimately
allowed science and mathematics to flourish.

Elizabeth Blackwell
1821-1910

Elizabeth was the first woman to qualify as a physician in America. She founded America's first medical school for women.

Elizabeth was the first woman to qualify as a physician in America. She founded America's first medical school for women.

Katharine Mccormick
1875-1967

Katharine McCormick was passionate about female empowerment and personally funded the first oral contraceptive, supervising its production from start to finish.

Katharine McCormick was passionate about female empowerment and personally funded the first oral contraceptive, supervising its production from start to finish.

Blaise Pascal
1623-1662

The French mathematician and physicist, Blaise Pascal, created the first calculator, named the Pascaline. He is likewise known for his modern theories of probabilities.

The French mathematician and physicist, Blaise Pascal, created the first calculator, named the Pascaline. He is likewise known for his modern theories of probabilities.

Charles Darwin
1809-1882

Charles Darwin coined the Theory of Evolution, which is the belief that every living thing comes from a common ancestor, and therefore all are related.

Charles Darwin coined the Theory of
Evolution, which is the belief that every
living thing comes from a common ancestor,
and therefore all are related.

Marie Curie
1867-1934

Marie Curie was the first woman to receive a Nobel Prize and the only woman to have ever received two. Both were for her work in radioactivity.

Marie Curie was the first woman to
receive a Nobel Prize and the only woman
to have ever received two. Both were for
her work in radioactivity.

Sau Lan Wu
1940s-Present

Hong Kong scientist Sau Lan Wu is a particle physicist who shaped the course of scientific history by being instrumental in the discovery of the Higgs boson particle.

Hong Kong scientist Sau Lan Wu is a
particle physicist who shaped the course of
scientific history by being instrumental in the
discovery of the Higgs boson particle.

Mary Anning
1799-1847

Mary Anning was a paleontologist who found her first fossil when she was just 12 years old. When she was 24, she discovered the first ever plesiosaur, a marine reptile fossil.

Mary Anning was a paleontologist who found her first fossil when she was just 12 years old. When she was 24, she discovered the first ever plesiosaur, a marine reptile fossil.

Rosalind Franklin
1920-1958

Rosalind Franklin discovered that DNA is shaped like a spiral. Her research lead to the famous X-Ray image, named Photo 51, that proved the structure of DNA is a helix.

Rosalind Franklin discovered that DNA is
shaped like a spiral. Her research lead to the
famous X-Ray image, named Photo 51, that
proved the structure of DNA is a helix.

Evangelista Torricelli
1608-1647

Mathematician and physicist Evangelista Torricelli built several telescopes and microscopes. He is most notably known for inventing the barometer, a tool that measures air pressure.

Mathematician and physicist Evangelista
Toricelli built several telescopes and
microscopes. He is most notably known
for inventing the barometer, a tool that
measures air pressure.

Grace Hopper
1906-1992

Pioneer of electronic computers. Invented the first compiler and was the principal architect of COBOL, the most widely used computer language of the twentieth century.

Pioneer of electronic computers. Invented the first compiler and was the principal architect of COBOL, the most widely used computer language of the twentieth century.

Lise Meitner
1878-1968

Lise Meitner was a physicist who, along with others, discovered nuclear fission. Despite her years of hard work, she was not awarded the Nobel Prize but her male partner was.

Lise Meitner was a physicist who, along with others, discovered nuclear fission. Despite her years of hard work, she was not awarded the Nobel Prize but her male partner was.

Johannes Kepler
1571-1630

Johannes Kepler discovered that the planets in our solar system travel around the sun in elliptical orbits, or oval-shaped paths. The orbit is also known as the "Kepler Orbit."

Johannes Kepler discovered that the
planets in our solar system travel around
the sun in elliptical orbits, or oval-shaped
paths. The orbit is also known as the
"Kepler Orbit."

Nicolaus Copernicus
1473-1543

Copernicus is known for his Heliocentric Model of the Universe. Copernicus controversially theorized that the sun was the center of the universe, rather than the Earth, as was the traditional belief.

Copernicus is known for his Heliocentric Model of the Universe. Copernicus controversially theorized that the sun was the center of the universe, rather than the Earth, as was traditional belief.

Jane Goodall
1937-Present

Jane Goodall discovered that chimpanzees make tools, eat, and hunt for meat, and have similar social behaviour to humans. She completely transformed our understanding of our closest relative in the animal kingdom.

Jane Goodall discovered that chimpanzees make tools, eat, and hunt for meat, and have similar social behaviour to humans. She completely transformed our understanding of our closest relative in the animal kingdom.

Vera Rubin
1928-2016

Vera Rubin discovered that invisible gravity sources were pulling planets and stars in certain directions, which proved that dark matter existed in the universe. She was awarded the National Medal of Science in 1993.

Vera Rubin discovered that invisible gravity sources were pulling planets and stars in certain directions, which proved that dark matter existed in the universe. She was awarded the National Medal of Science in 1993.

Caroline Herschel
1750-1848

Herschel was a brilliant astronomer from England, who discovered new nebulae and star clusters. She was the first female scientist to discover a comet and the first to have her work published by the Royal Society.

Herschel was a brilliant astronomer from England, who discovered new nebulae and star clusters. She was the first female scientist to discover a comet and the first to have her work published by the Royal Society.

Alexander Graham Bell
1847-1922

Bell is most famous for inventing the telephone. Both his wife and his mother were hearing impaired, which is what sparked his interest in sound and lead him to experiment in channeling sound waves through wires.

Bell is most famous for inventing the telephone. Both his wife and his mother were hearing impaired, which is what sparked his interest in sound and lead him to experiment in channeling sound waves through wires.

Rita Levi-Montalcini
1909-2012

Rita Levi-Montalcini was a 1986 Nobel Prize winner for her discovery of the nerve growth factor. Rita's work paved the way for breakthroughs on how anomalies in nerve growth affect diseases like dementia and cancer.

Rita Levi-Montalcini was a 1986 Nobel Prize winner for her discovery of the nerve growth factor. Rita's work paved the way for breakthroughs on how anomalies in nerve growth affect diseases like dementia and cancer.

Barbara McClintock
1902-1992

Scientist Barbara McClintock discovered that genes are mobile, meaning they can change position on the chromosome. She began her work by studying corn, and how its appearance changed over consecutive generations.

Scientist Barbara McClintock discovered that genes are mobile, meaning they can change position on the chromosome. She began her work by studying corn, and how its appearance changed over consecutive generations.

Archimedes
287 BC - 212 BC

Founder of mechanics and hydrostatics sciences, Archimedes was responsible for precisely calculating the value of pi, devising the law of exponents, creating new geometrical proofs and many various mechanical inventions.

Founder of mechanics and hydrostatics
sciences, Archimedes was responsible for
precisely calculating the value of pi,
devising the law of exponents, creating new
geometrical proofs and many various
mechanical inventions.

Jennifer Doudna

1964-Present

Jennifer Doudna's life of study has been instrumental in developing treatment for sickle cell anemia, cystic fibrosis, Huntington's disease, and HIV. In 2020 she received the Nobel Prize in Chemistry for the "development of a method for genome editing."

Jennifer Doudna's life of study has been instrumental in developing treatment for sickle cell anemia, cystic fibrosis, Huntington's disease, and HIV. In 2020 she received the Nobel Prize in Chemistry for the "development of a method for genome editing."

Carl Linnaeus
1707-1778

In the early days plants and animals had common names that varied across regions and languages, as well as "phrase names" and inconvenient Latin descriptions. Linnaeus devised the binomial nomenclature system that has given the world clarity for naming living things.

In the early days plants and animals had
common names that varied across regions
and languages, as well as "phrase names" and
inconvenient Latin descriptions. Linnaeus
devised the binomial nomenclature system
that has given the world clarity for naming
living things.

Edward Jenner
1749-1823

In 1821 Edward Jenner was appointed as the official physician to King George. Often called the "Father of Immunology," Edward Jenner pioneered the smallpox vaccine. Over the last couple of centuries, Jenner's research in vaccinations has saved countless lives all over the world.

In 1821 Edward Jenner was appointed as
the official physician to King George. Often
called the "Father of Immunology," Edward
Jenner pioneered the smallpox vaccine. Over
the last couple of centuries, Jenner's research
in vaccinations has saved countless lives all
over the world.

Anders Celsius
1701-1744

Anders Celsius was a Swedish astronomer and professor who studied temperature and proposed the Celsius scale for temperatures. Celsius likewise studied the connection between the aurora borealis and the Earth's magnetic field. He has published findings that indicated Scandinavia was rising above sea level.

Anders Celsius was a Swedish astronomer
and professor who studied temperature and
proposed the Celsius scale for temperatures.
Celsius likewise studied the connection
between the aurora borealis and the Earth's
magnetic field. He has published findings that
indicated Scandinavia was rising above
sea level.

James Watt
1736-1819

James Watt was a Scottish mechanical engineer and inventor who improved the efficiency of the steam engine, with the use of an independent condenser and parallel motion. Watt likewise developed the idea of horsepower. Most notably, the electrical unit "watt" is named after him.

James Watt was a Scottish mechanical
engineer and inventor who improved the
efficiency of the steam engine, with the use
of an independent condenser and parallel
motion. Watt likewise developed the idea of
horsepower. Most notably, the electrical unit
"watt" is named after him.

Thomas Edison
1847-1931

Thomas Edison was the creator of some of the most prominent technologies that are used in most households today. This includes the electric light bulb, phonograph and motion pictures, among many others. As such, he held more than a thousand patents for his inventions.

Thomas Edison was the creator of some of
the most prominent technologies that are
used in most households today. This includes
the electric light bulb, phonograph and motion
pictures, among many others. As such, he
held more than a thousand patents for his
inventions.

Galileo Galilei
1564-1642

Known as the "Discoverer of the Cosmos," Italian mathematician Galileo Galilei pointed a telescope at the moon and from there founded modern astronomy. His conclusions proved the theories of Copernicus' solar system model. He is also known for his law of inertia, explaining the Earth's rotation.

Known as the "Discoverer of the Cosmos,"
Italian mathematician Galileo Galilei pointed
a telescope at the moon and from there
founded modern astronomy. His conclusions
proved the theories of Copernicus' solar
system model. He is also known for his law
of inertia, explaining the Earth's rotation.

Marie Tharp
1920-2006

Geologist and cartographer Marie Tharp explored the oceans from her Columbia University desk. She revealed a landscape of mountain ranges and deep trenches on Earth's seafloor. Her keen eye likewise spotted the first indications of underwater plate tectonics, and her observations have become crucial to proving continental drift.

Geologist and cartographer Marie Tharp
explored the oceans from her Columbia
University desk. She revealed a landscape
of mountain ranges and deep trenches on
Earth's seafloor. Her keen eye likewise
spotted the first indications of underwater
plate tectonics, and her observations have
become crucial to proving continental drift.

Tycho Brahe
1546-1601

Tycho Brahe was a Danish astronomer known for his comprehensive observations in astronomy. He proposed the Tychonic Model, stating that the Earth is stationary and is the center of the planetary system. While the sun and the moon revolved around the Earth, the other planets revolved around the sun.

Tycho Brahe was a Danish astronomer
known for his comprehensive observations
in astronomy. He proposed the Tychonic
Model, stating that the Earth is stationary
and is the center of the planetary system.
While the sun and the moon revolved around
the Earth, the other planets revolved around
the sun.

Gertrude Elion
1918-1999

Nobel Prize awardee Gertrude Elion was an American biochemist and pharmacologist who developed drugs for the treatment of leukemia and the prevention of kidney transplant rejection. As a teenager, Gertrude watched her grandfather die of cancer and from then on devoted her life to studying how to fight the disease.

Nobel Prize awardee Gertrude Elion was an
American biochemist and pharmacologist who
developed drugs for the treatment of
leukemia and the prevention of kidney
transplant rejection. As a teenager, Gertrude
watched her grandfather die of cancer and
from then on devoted her life to studying
how to fight the disease.

William Thomson Kelvin
1824-1907

British physicist and engineer, William Thomson Kelvin, determined the value for absolute zero in the study of temperature, bringing forth the Kelvin scale of temperature. Kelvin likewise estimated the Earth's age to be between 20 and 400 million years old. Kelvin was key in developing the second law of thermodynamics.

British physicist and engineer, William
Thomson Kelvin, determined the value for
absolute zero in the study of temperature,
bringing forth the Kelvin scale of temperature.
Kelvin likewise estimated the Earth's age to
be between 20 and 400 million years old.
Kelvin was key in developing the second law
of thermodynamics.

Alfred Nobel
1824-1896

Alfred Nobel was a Swedish scientist who invented dynamite. In modern times, Alfred Nobel is best known for the Nobel Prizes, which are named after him and generally granted to individuals who are exceptional in their work in the sciences, such as those who have made significant discoveries or inventions in their respective fields.

Alfred Nobel was a Swedish scientist who invented dynamite. In modern times, Alfred Nobel is best known for the Nobel Prizes, which are named after him and generally granted to individuals who are exceptional in their work in the sciences, such as those who have made significant discoveries or inventions in their respective fields.

Stephen Hawking
1942-2018

Stephen Hawking was an English theoretical physicist, cosmologist and author. His books showcase the range and boldness of his ideas: The Universe in a Nutshell and The Theory of Everything. Hawking once declared that his goal was simply to achieve "a complete understanding of the universe, why it is as it is and why it exists at all."

Stephen Hawking was an English theoretical physicist, cosmologist and author. His books showcase the range and boldness of his ideas: The Universe in a Nutshell and The Theory of Everything. Hawking once declared that his goal was simply to achieve "a complete understanding of the universe, why it is as it is and why it exists at all."

Mileva Marić
1875-1948

Mileva Marić was a Serbian physicist and mathematician. She was married to Albert Einstein from 1903-1919. Marić was known for modeling the woman's role in science, as she broke traditions in academic institutions across Europe. Her actual contributions to Einstein's work have been widely debated, particularly over the Annus Mirabilis Papers of 1905.

Mileva Marić was a Serbian physicist and mathematician. She was married to Albert Einstein from 1903-1919. Marić was known for modeling the woman's role in science, as she broke traditions in academic institutions across Europe. Her actual contributions to Einstein's work have been widely debated, particularly over the Annus Mirabilis Papers of 1905.

Gregor Mendel
1822-1884

Known as the Father of Modern Genetics, Gregor Mendel was an Austrian scientist who experimented with hybridizations in plants. Mendel discovered that many of his findings with plants could be applied to animals and humans. It was in his in-depth study of genetics that he came to coin the terms "recessive" and "dominant" when referring to genes.

Known as the Father of Modern Genetics, Gregor Mendel was an Austrian scientist who experimented with hybridizations in plants. Mendel discovered that many of his findings with plants could be applied to animals and humans. It was in his in-depth study of genetics that he came to coin the terms "recessive" and "dominant" when referring to genes.

James Clerk Maxwell
1831-1879

James Clerk Maxwell was a Scottish mathematician and scientist, who was the lead proponent for the classical theory of electromagnetic radiation. This was the first theory to describe electricity, magnetism and light as the various manifestations of the same phenomenon. James Clerk Maxwell also made fundamental contributions to the fields of mathematics, astronomy and engineering.

James Clerk Maxwell was a Scottish

mathematician and scientist, who was the

lead proponent for the classical theory of

electromagnetic radiation. This was the first

theory to describe electricity, magnetism and

light as the various manifestations of the

same phenomenon. James Clerk Maxwell

also made fundamental contributions to the

fields of mathematics, astronomy and
engineering.

Alan Turing
1912-1954

Alan Turing was a British mathematician, computer scientist, logician and cryptanalyst. During World War II, Alan Turing worked for Britain creating ciphers that helped decode German messages. He has been regarded as the Father of Artificial Intelligence, and a pioneer in theoretical computer science. He formalised the concepts of algorithm and computation with the Turing Machine.

Alan Turing was a British mathematician,
computer scientist, logician and cryptanalyst.
During World War II, Alan Turing worked for
Britain creating ciphers that helped decode
German messages. He has been regarded
as the Father of Artificial Intelligence, and a
pioneer in theoretical computer science. He
formalised the concepts of algorithm and

computation with the Turing Machine.

108

Dmitri Mendeleev
1834-1907

A Russian chemist, Dmitri Mendeleev, is best known for creating the iconic Periodic Table, the standard reference used across the world to this day. In 1869, Mendeleev published "Principles of Chemistry," which details his work in arranging the various elements according to their atomic mass. Mendeleev is also credited for introducing the metric system to the Russian Empire.

A Russian chemist, Dmitri Mendeleev, is best

known for creating the iconic Periodic Table,

the standard reference used across the world

to this day. In 1869, Mendeleev published

"Principles of Chemistry," which details his work

in arranging the various elements according

to their atomic mass. Mendeleev is also

credited for introducing the metric system

to the Russian Empire.

Louis Pasteur
1822-1895

Louis Pasteur was an influential figure in the field of medical microbiology. Besides discovering the process of pasteurization, he devoted much of his life's work to finding cures for diseases and devising methods for reducing the harmful bacteria in milk, wine and other produce. He discovered the vaccine for anthrax and rabies. His work was also instrumental in reducing the mortality rates from puerperal fever.

Louis Pasteur was an influential figure in the
field of medical microbiology. Besides
discovering the process of pasteurization, he
devoted much of his life's work to finding
cures for diseases and devising methods for
reducing the harmful bacteria in milk, wine and
other produce. He discovered the vaccine for
anthrax and rabies. His work was also

instrumental in reducing the mortality rates from puerperal fever.

Leonardo da Vinci
1452-1519

Leonardo da Vinci was an Italian Renaissance thinker who is credited for several inventions and discoveries in the fields of engineering, anatomy, and hydrodynamics. He designed the Aerial Screw, which was an early precursor to the principle of the modern helicopter. Da Vinci was one of the most well-known artists in history, and his most notable works of art include the Mona Lisa, The Last Supper and the Virtuvian Man.

Leonardo da Vinci was an Italian Renaissance
thinker who is credited for several inventions
and discoveries in the fields of engineering,
anatomy and hydrodynamics. He designed
the Aerial Screw, which was an early precursor
to the principle of the modern helicopter.
Da Vinci was one of the most well-known
artists in history, and his most notable works

of art include the Mona Lisa, The Last
Supper and The Virtuvian Man.

Nikola Tesla
1856-1943

Nikola Tesla was a Serbian-American engineer and inventor who is best known for his development of alternating current (AC) electrical systems. This eccentric genius, who once claimed to have accidentally caused an earthquake with a steam-powered electric generator he'd invented, is now known as a "Wizard of Industrial Revolution." Tesla's designs advanced alternating current during the electric age, and allowed utilities to transmit electrical current over expansive distances. He developed the Tesla coil — a high-voltage transformer — and techniques to wirelessly transmit power. The world's most famous electric car bears his name.

Nikola Tesla was a Serbian-American engineer and inventor who is best known for his development of alternating current (AC) electrical systems. This eccentric genius, who once claimed to have accidentally caused an earthquake with a steam-powered electric generator he'd invented, is now known as a "Wizard of Industrial Revolution." Tesla's designs advanced alternating current during the electric age, and allowed utilities to transmit electrical current over expansive distances. He developed the Tesla coil--a high-voltage transformer--and techniques to wirelessly transmit power. The world's most famous electric car bears his name.

Hi there! This book was created just for you, to help you improve your handwriting in a fun and meaningful way. We would love to hear about it as you write a short review on Amazon. It could really help us.

If you have any questions about this book, please feel free to contact Leslie Mars at:

Lesliemarsbooks@gmail.com

Printed in Great Britain
by Amazon